Grayson's
Art Club

The
Exhibition

CW00377164

Grayson's Art Club: The Exhibition

Exhibition supported by Channel 4
and Swan Films

Curator: Grayson Perry, Natasha Howes
and Fiona Corridan
Editor: Charles McKenzie
Design: Alice Fraser, Craig Oldham,
Office Of Craig
Printing: Pression

First published in 2020 by Manchester Art
Gallery, Mosley Street, Manchester M2 3JL
manchesterartgallery.org

© Swan Films, Manchester Art Gallery
and the authors

Image credits: Grayson's Art Club stills
courtesy of Swan Films. All other images
Michael Pollard unless otherwise stated

More information about the exhibition
can be found at: manchesterartgallery.org/
exhibitions-andevents/exhibition/graysons-
art-club/

Any copy of this book issued by the publisher
is sold subject to the condition that it shall
not by way of trade or otherwise be lent,
re-sold, hired out or otherwise circulated
without the publisher's prior consent in any
form of binding or cover other than that in
which it is published and without a similar
condition including these words being
imposed on a subsequent purchaser.

All Rights Reserved. No part of this
publication may be reproduced or transmitted
in any form or by any means, electronic or
mechanical, including photocopy, recording
or any other information storage and retrieval
system, without prior permission in writing
from the publisher.

A catalogue record for this book is available
from the British Library.

ISBN 978-0-9016739-9-2

Welcome to Art Club

Foreword

Alistair Hudson
Director
Manchester Art Gallery

Art is for everyone

Manchester Art Gallery has witnessed many significant events since its founding in 1823. It has seen wars, civil unrest, depressions, disease and political upheaval. Its collections of art, craft, design and dress reflect this history, and, like all museums, it is a place where we collectively write the story of our society.

2020 will be remembered for the global catastrophe of the Coronavirus pandemic, for the lives it has taken and what it has taken from life. The lockdown was the first time the Gallery has been forced to close its doors to the public in a history that spans three centuries. Across the country and around the world other public institutions were also shut; the places and spaces we inhabit and share our humanity with other people, became out of reach. Locked in isolation, huge numbers sought physical, sensory stimulation in whatever way they could: cooking, gardening, singing, painting, film-making, potting and pottering. Unable to commune with the muses in the museum, they sought them out in their living room. In solitude, we rediscovered the value of art.

Through our screens, *Grayson's Art Club* brought the country together during lockdown, celebrating this creativity in people's homes across the land. It captured perfectly the way many people have found solace in making, and expressed this with humour, pathos and imagination.

The programme clearly demonstrates how people create art as an essential part of their lives. In this way, *Art Club's* ethos chimes perfectly with that of Manchester Art Gallery, rooted in our long-held purpose to be an art school for everyone and to promote the uses of art in the making of a healthy society.

We are immensely happy that Grayson, Channel 4 and Swan Films chose Manchester Art Gallery as the venue to present the exhibition of the series, and to choose Manchester as the place for this national celebration of artistic talent. We anticipate that the exhibition will be hugely popular and will help the Gallery rebuild itself after the devastation of the last year. It will also play a key part in the re-building of society post-Covid, bringing life and soul, back into the city.

Finally I wish to pay tribute and say thanks to all the artists in the exhibition, who have so eloquently narrated this chapter in the cultural story.

Introduction
Grayson Perry

Art will
help us
through these
tough times

Looking through images of the artworks we have selected to be part of this exhibition, I am taken aback by how flushed with pride I feel, not just for the beauty, skill, charm and fun in the art but even more so for the breadth of people who are part of this. My favourite thing about *Art Club* is that we managed to talk to and show artists from right across the spectrum of who it is that loves to make visual art. From world famous established professionals like Maggi Hambling or Antony Gormley, to comedians who take art very seriously like Jim Moir or Harry Hill. From art students, emerging artists through enthusiastic amateurs, old and young, to self-confessed complete novices like Clare Warde whose painting of the bins from her window will forever sum up lockdown for me, one of them emblazoned with the graffiti 'Nut's About Life'.

Back in March 2020, as soon as lockdown seemed imminent, Neil Crombie, my friend, director and collaborator, said 'We need to do something, people are going to be stuck at home, they will need something to do.' And so *Art Club* was conceived. Normally when we make television together we might take a year of musing, plotting and researching before we embarked on a series. With *Art Club* it was barely a month! One advantage of lockdown was that many of the best technicians, editors, composers were suddenly very available! I am not a great believer in the artistic cliché of the flash of inspiration and the frenzy of creation but *Art Club* came together very fast and it worked, not least because we had a great team. Everyone involved has been so chuffed at the positive reception to *Art Club*, hardly a day goes by when Philippa or I am not approached in the street (at a safe distance of course) and told how much the series meant to people during that initial scary lonely lockdown.

I am the first to admit that making art becomes a very different thing once you commit to becoming an 'artist' and pursuing a career as a professional, but it does not change the fundamental process or the pleasure (and pain!) that can come from trying to make a satisfying image. *Art Club* has reminded me in a visceral way that a huge part of the joy is in losing yourself in the making, being involved, being vulnerable. This pleasure is available to all, even someone like visually impaired Emma Major who, I can say with confidence having met her, exudes joy like few others.

Making art has always been an immense comfort to me. From childhood I have found that I can venture off into that creative part of myself and feel safe and in control, absorbed. Distressing things could be happening all around but I could always retreat into a mental state where I was in charge even if it was of only a box of Lego or a pencil and paper. The therapeutic role of art making so movingly illustrated by Alex Robinson and his vast cast of characters from his imaginary *ComputerWorld*, to which he adds four more, every Saturday, without fail.

I have always thought it was those who make art who get the most out of it. Looking at art is lovely; it can be challenging, upsetting, moving, funny, but in creating it, we tap into our ability to turn our thoughts, feelings, skills and ideas into images. In making art we communicate in a very particular way; often it is our unconscious talking to the viewer's unconscious. Beware, this is powerful. I am often surprised by what I have let slip about myself in my art and looking at the thousands of submissions to *Art Club,* I can say I am not alone!

All of my life art has been integral to maintaining and exploring my own mental health – it has helped me externalise who I am, where I have been and where I would like to go. Between you and me I don't think *Art Club* is principally about art. It's mostly about people, telling their stories with images, individual stories, their family stories, community stories and the stories that they share with all of us. I will never forget how touched I was by Paul Green telling us how fashioning his wire sculptures of garden birds helped him cope with being unable to go to his beloved nature reserve where he worked. I was lucky enough to have an expert on stories by my side throughout *Art Club*. My biggest influence and source of wisdom has always been my wife Philippa but never before has being married to a psychotherapist for thirty years come in so handy!

I was adamant from the offset that this exhibition would not be staged in London. I love London, I live there, it's where the centre of the British art world resides but *Art Club* is not just for the Art World, it is for the whole country. I also wanted it to be held in a grand venue, somewhere that all the artists would be delighted to see there their work hanging. So Manchester Art Gallery fulfills this brief perfectly. My only sadness is that I was hoping for a big opening party where everyone could celebrate and mingle but it was not to be.

I am so grateful to all the artists who opened up to me and who showed their work on national television. I am also grateful to them for generously lending to this exhibition which runs for a considerable time. Thanks to everyone at Swan Films, Channel Four and Manchester Art Gallery.

We were all in shock. A pandemic was a situation none of us had lived through before. Several months later the 'new normal' doesn't feel so new any more! I hope that this exhibition cheers and touches you in these bleak times and inspires you to make art for yourself and for the world and maybe the next series of *Art Club*!

Grayson

traits

Chantal Joffe

Artist

Grayson Perry: Chantal Joffe is a portrait artist whose work I really like. A couple of years ago she embarked on a project to paint a self-portrait every single day for a year, which seems like the perfect preparation for lockdown.

Here's someone who's done portraits all of her career. She seemed to really understand the pure essence of what it is, that kind of 'in the now' observing a sort of unforgivingness but also acceptance of what you're looking at. An interesting lesson and the fact that her project of doing a portrait every day for a year was very healing for her, you know, and we're all in a wounded situation. So, get painting, get portraiting.

It's good for you.

What is the best thing about working from home?

Chantal Joffe: I like the way time feels endless, it sort of floats around. That's a really nice thing but it makes you ask what it is you're doing and that's a really good thing if you're trying to be an artist, it's to ask yourself, 'Why am I doing this?' Rather than somehow taking it for granted, you're right to do it or what you're doing. So, I guess that's the best thing about working from home.

For me painting is a constant in my life, I've painted myself probably since I was about, I don't know, six. You know, I'm always here, aren't I, and I really only like painting people. Often it's just me, so that's a good place to start. I think a lot of the time I forget it's me that I'm painting. You sort of zoom in and out, I guess, of a

consciousness of it being a self-portrait. I was curious if I would look different, if the awful stuff that's happening would be somehow reflected in my face but, of course, I won't know that until later.

GP: *What advice would you give to other people who wanted to start making art from home?*
CJ: I would say not to make it hard for yourself. I'd say that you have to make it as possible as you can. So if you've got a pencil and some print paper like photocopy paper you can do a drawing and I'd say, 'Okay, let that be enough for then.' It seems to me that the whole virtue of lockdown is the economy we're all gonna be forced to use, so when I run out of paint and if the shops run out of paint, or they shut them or can't

get paint, then I'll draw with pastels and when they run out it'll be pencils and then it'll be biro, and maybe the work will get better out of the economy. I believe in that. I believe the best art is where the most economical means to get to what you want is actually always the best.

Previous:
Lockdown Self-Portrait
in my Nightie
2020

Chantal Joffe

Oil on board
Courtesy the artist
and Victoria Miro

Nathan Wyburn

Artist

Nathan Wyburn: I make celebrity portraits by using things that I can find around the house.

If you just want to make some art around the house, you can basically just raid the cupboards, find that old tin of beans or can of spaghetti at the back of the cupboard, and maybe a half empty bottle of tomato ketchup. I actually love the noodles that I placed in on the end of the Grayson Perry portrait because it adds such a 3D and sculptural element to the final work and the way the soy sauce actually grips to the noodles then gives that extra dark tone around the hair, which I really need to make the portrait jump out of the paper.

Previous:
Grayson Perry
2020

Nathan Wyburn

Soya sauce and noodles
on paper
Courtesy of the artist

Pasta

Wars!

Stay at Home!
2020

Penny Lally

Bronze resin on wood base
Courtesy of the artist

"STAY AT HOME"

Lockdown Self-Portrait
2020

Bethan Barlow

Acrylic on canvas
Courtesy of the artist

"I love that. I like the kind of
oddness of the shape of the
eyes, there's such a lot of life
in it. It made me happy
when I saw it."

Joe Lycett

Celebrity
Pick

Generation COVID
2020

Lucilda Goulden–White

Acrylic on board
Courtesy of the artist

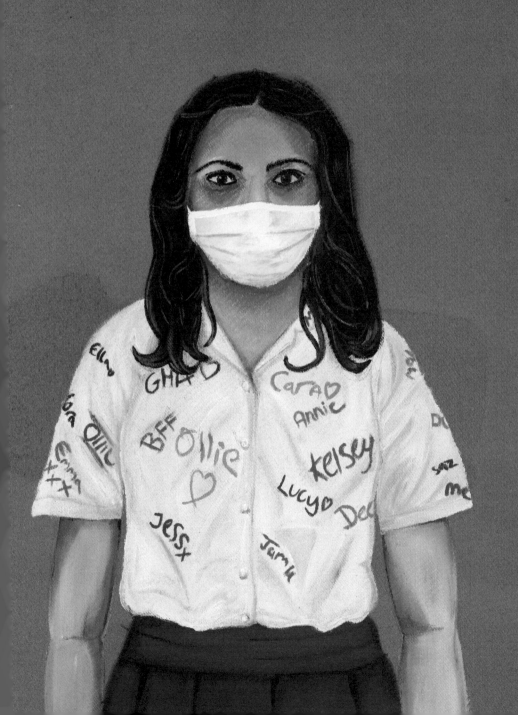

Aquaria
2020

Miranda Noszkiewicz

Acrylic on canvas
Courtesy of the artist

"When you're putting together
an exhibition you want
something that's really gonna
stand out and Miranda's
portrait I think has that ability,
and I kind of like drag queens."

Grayson Perry

Grayson's
Pick

Mama
2020

Kashta Dale

Digital painting
Courtesy of the artist

Arthur
2020

Linda Hann

Clay
Courtesy of the artist

"Yeah, it's quite a, you know,
interesting looking head."

Joe Lycett

Celebrity Pick

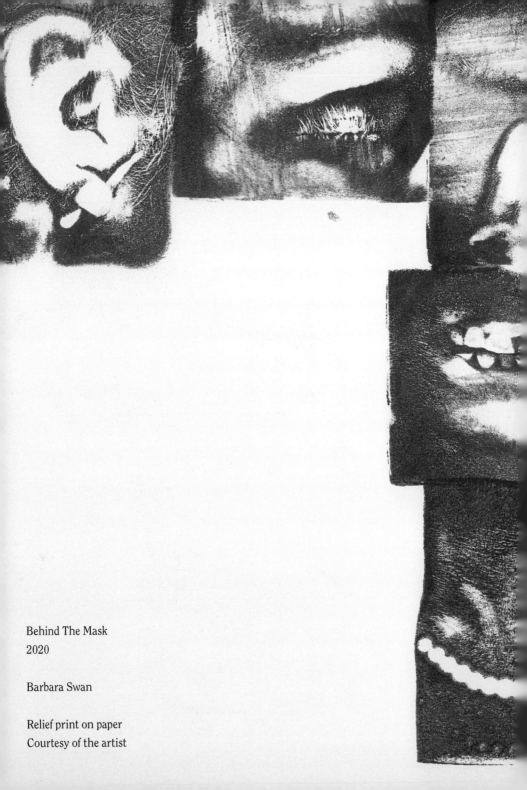

Behind The Mask
2020

Barbara Swan

Relief print on paper
Courtesy of the artist

The Last Supper
2020

Henry Mawcat

Oil on canvas board
Courtesy of the artist

"I think it's absolutely brilliant.
I saw that and I was like,
That's one of my favourite
paintings I've ever seen.
I want it in my house, I think
it's so funny."

Joe Lycett

Celebrity Pick

Mutual Appreciation in
Isolation:
Dad and Dog
2020

Emily Goodden

Acrylic on paper
Courtesy of the artist

Family Portrait
2020

Philippa Perry

Glazed ceramic
Courtesy of the artist

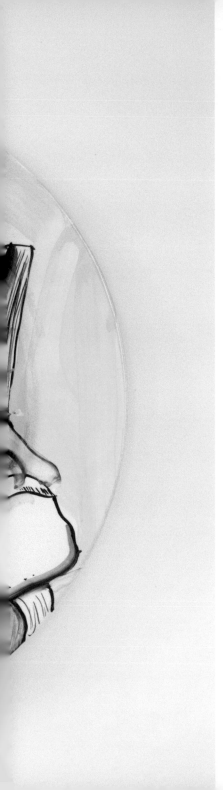

A Portrait of Phillipa
2020

Grayson Perry

Ceramic Plate
Courtesy of the artist
and Victoria Miro

"Because I'm painting my
wife of 30 years or so, she is
often the first pair of eyes
who sees anything that I
make. So I want her to like
it. It's been a while since
I've done a portrait of Phil.
It does make you think
about your relationship with
them. Perhaps now is an
opportunity for us all
to spend some time
reflecting on those we're
in lockdown with."

Grayson Perry

WASH

YOUR FILTHY
PIG HANDS

Joe Lycett

The Itty Bitty Chris Whitty
Committee
2020

Hugo Boss (now known as
Joe Lycett)

Acrylic paint
Oil paint
Watercolour paint
Farrow & Ball paint
Linseed oil
Olive oil
Soil
Boiled soil
Boiled oil
Boiled oiled olive oil soil
A drop of sweet, crisp water
from a summer well
The breath of a dying quail
Sandpaper from a Norwich
branch of Wickes
A kitten's first memory
Alan Sugar
Greggs Steak Bake
Greg's Greggs Steak Bake
A Greggs Steak Bake Cake
Greg's Greggs Steak Bake
Cake
Anish Kapoor's grazed shins
A knob of salted butter in the
palm of a dentist
Harry Styles' harried stylists
1.532
Miaow
A cool breeze sprinkling over
the a-line skirt of a mid-tier
estate agent called Sandra
A birthday type two
diabetes diagnosis

A king's blouse
A queen's sheath
A prince's pocket watch
Two dozen unanswered
emails from Manchester
University begging for money
Alan Sugar
A mother's knuckle
Goat's milk
Ghost's milk
Ghost goat's milk
A wicker chair's leg in
the mouth of a pigeon
A haystack in a needle
Seven fresh piglets
Lettuce leaves
Let us leave
Alan Sugar
A rounded up number
no larger than 8.4
Ruth Langsford's
secret notepad
Wales
A pane of glass in the shape
of my knob
16 random DMs from JK
Rowling's twitter account
A 1120 Continental bin filled
with thick double cream
32 years of hopes and dreams
Alan Sugar
A sense that something
is missing
A thin piece of tissue paper,
torn in one corner,
signifying nothing
Alan Sugar
Alan Sugar
Alan Sugar
Alan Sugar

Alan Sugar
Alan Sugar
Alan Sugar
Alan Sugar
Alen Shughart
A reduced price canvas
I bought in a Birmingham
branch of The Works

Courtesy of the artist

Chris
Whitty is
Watching
YOU!

Portraiture with Joe Lycett

Joe Lycett: I have obviously my brushes, I have some water, a plate, my canvas, which seems to have stuck to something, and loads of paints.

The key thing that I find when we're doing portraits is, I don't care about a likeness at all. I just literally just try and recreate the shape of it and then the monk hair kind of comes out there. It's quite a look, the monk hair. Having hair like that is as bold as going out in drag, I think, because it's mad. You look mad. There's nothing wrong with that.

Now, what I'm going to do is I'm going to make a skin tone. So you get a little bit of yellow, a little bit of red. Just put a dollop of white in there, maybe a drop more red and then I will just literally give it a coat of this because I find with acrylics once you get a coat and it's dried a bit you've got something to work with. Now one thing that I was really drawn to about Chris is his eyes. He's got extraordinary eyes. So, now what I'm doing is I'm literally just looking at where's the bits of red, where's there bits of light, and I'm literally just dolloping it on.

I imagine that very skilled portrait painters are seeing this going, 'Oh.' I know when a painting is going well for me when I start laughing at it. I'm gonna try his nose now. Oh, there's a nostril. I mean, I've just gone straight on in there.

I mean, there he is. The Chief Medical Officer, Chris Whitty.

Grayson Perry: How is it being in lockdown being a comedian?
JL: To be honest, people are generally held at a distance from me. You know I'm never that close to the general public really, thank God. Literally so full of germs right now. It is strange not seeing family and friends but actually I do feel like I've connected with them a lot better than I have done in a long time because we're doing these games nights and whatever, and really make an effort to see one another.

GP: Tell me why you have chosen Morning Sun by Edward Hopper *as your favourite portrait.*
JL: I'm not a sad person particularly but I love calm and quiet, and that painting for me is peaceful and it just soothes me. I've tried to paint similar things but because I'm nowhere near as skilled as Hopper, or any of these people, they end up looking just a bit naff and I got cross with that. And so I always revert back to doing silly things and my art is always silly because then if things go wrong, I can blame it on, 'Oh, that was what I was meant to do because I'm a silly person and everything has to be silly.' But actually I would really love to be able to paint really beautifully calm things.

Blank

Canvas

Animals

Maggi Hambling

Artist

Maggi Hambling: In a way nothing has changed. I still come into the studio very early every morning, 5:00 or 6:00 and first of all make a drawing rather like a pianist practicing the scales, just to renew that sense of touch and then get on with whatever bundle of trouble is on that painting wall. In the afternoons, if life were at all normal, I would watch some tennis and then the early evening take a can of special brew to what I call 'the sunset bench'. I'm not a park bench drinker of special brew, I'm a sunset bench drinker of special brew.

This painting is called *March 2020*. It's the contradiction of the threat of the virus all around us but all around us was spring, things suddenly coming into blossom, the life force of nature and

so this painting is a vulnerable rising blossom of magnolia with the creeping greys of the virus threatening its life. Getting up as I do very early every morning, I always hear the dawn chorus but throughout the day you hear much more birdsong and all around us, as I say, everything coming into bloom and blossom, and that joy and so that contradiction is what this painting is about.

My work is my life and my life is my work. My great teacher, the artist Lett-Haines, said the most important thing that anyone has ever said to me is, 'If you're going to be an artist, you must make your work your best friend.' In other words you can go to it whatever you're feeling, if you're feeling tired,

you're feeling bored, you're feeling happy, you're feeling randy, whatever you're feeling, go to your work and have a conversation with it. So, that is how I live my life. The time in this studio is real, it's real time and time is all one has. I feel most alive when I'm in this studio trying to make something and I think an artist's best way of giving love really is in their work.

Grayson Perry: If you were to give some advice to somebody about how to approach art and making art in this current situation, what would you say?
MH: Well, I'd say the same as I'd say without the current situation, to make a drawing every day and to look at the great masters. If you draw every day, most people have got half an hour when

they're not worried about their fridge freezer or something, then it becomes like breathing, drawing being like one's handwriting, I mean, the most intimate thing that one does. I get pottier than ever if for some reason I'm ill or something and don't do it for a couple of days. I go pottier than ever, of course it's therapy. We're very lucky.

Previous:
March 2020
2020

Maggi Hambling

Oil on canvas
Courtesy of the artist
and Marlborough

Kevin

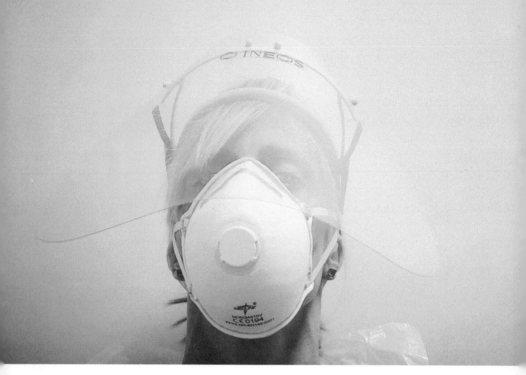

Overleaf:
Dog Show
Above:
Selfie at Work in PPE
Top Right:
The New Normal
Bottom Right:
Swings in Lockdown
2020

Hannah Grace Deller

Photographs
Courtesy of the artist

"It's all very touching to think someone like Hannah who is at the frontline of the crisis we're all going through, even she finds solace in taking photographs and pictures of animals, and isn't that an amazing thing?"

Grayson Perry

Grayson's Pick

Pandemic Penguin Parade
2020

Hannah Hill &
Eshe Deodat-Hill

Mixed media (Felt,
embroidery thread,
glass beads, plastic,
velvet and paint)

Courtesy of the artists

Billy
2020

Anne Bridgeman

Gouache paint and
watercolour pencils
Courtesy of the artist

"I like the fact that it's floating
in the sky, sort of like he's
come down."

Harry Hill

Celebrity Pick

Lockdown Birds
2020

Paul Green

Wire
Courtesy of the artist

Annie Dog
2020

Hollie Arnett

Acrylic on card
Courtesy of the artist

"I think if Hollie had filled in
the details it would only be
half the painting. I have this
kind of think about people
who won't do art, so many
people are self-conscious but
I really urge people to have
a go at it."

Harry Hill

Celebrity
Pick

Emu in Lockdown
2020

Liza Donoghue

Acrylic on canvas
Courtesy of the artist

Lulu
2020

Jill Dudley

Gouache on watercolour paper
Courtesy Jane Cummings

Lulu x

2020

Our Pets
2020

Susan Hubbard and
Tyler Brown

Acrylic on canvas
Courtesy of the artists

"I think you've got lockdown
right there, haven't you?
Crowded in the room, a big
family all fighting for air.
It's distinctive and it doesn't
remind me of any other
particular painter."

Harry Hill

Trevor
2020

Sharon Bennett

Watercolour on paper
Courtesy of the artist

Previous:
Acid Mouse and Sexy Cooking
Apple with cars for shoes
2020

Noel Fielding

Oil stick on black paper
Courtesy of the artist

Cats I, II and III
2020

Phillipa Perry

Glazed ceramics
Courtesy of the artist

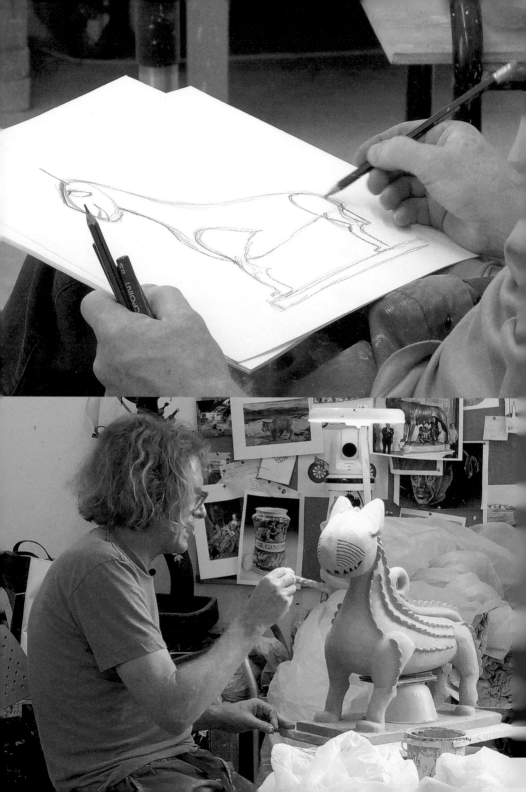

Chris Whitty's Cat
2020

Grayson Perry

Cast silver
Courtesy of the artist and
Victoria Miro

"I was looking through
sculptures of cats and a
sculpture that really caught
my eye was an Islamic
incense burner. I just loved
the elegant shape of it so
I'm looking at that and
thinking how I might use
that shape to make a kind
of quiet little domestic scale
monument to the crisis
we're going through.
So, that's what I'm gonna
make, plague cat."

Grayson Perry

Harry Hill

Wood Carving with Harry Hill

Harry Hill: 'There's a dog in every log. In every log.'

So, what I've decided to do is carve a dog and it's based on a golden retriever who was found swimming between the Isle of Wight and Portsmouth. The first part is just getting as much as possible off the log to expose the dog within.

I took it in to show the family and the main comment was it looks too much like a teddy bear. It does a bit. So, what we're gonna do is take a bit off the top.

This is what we've got so far and as you can see I've used a bit of wood filler to fill in the nose just to give him a slightly less teddy bear-ish profile and I've added that all-important tail. Now I'm gonna sand down the wood filler with some sand paper and I've also found a couple of glass eyes which I've been saving.

So this is our friend and what I'm gonna do now is I'm gonna paint him.

And there we have, Soloman.

Grayson Perry: How are you coping with lockdown Harry?
HH: You know what? I think I prefer it, in some ways. I was thinking the other day what does it remind me of? Quiet, less traffic, the birds in the sky, not much to do and it reminds me of the 70s.

And normally I hate not working but if no one else is working, that's fine.

I've been doing gigs, I did a couple of gigs online. It's just like you basically shouting at your laptop. There was a link up to the front row so you could see them. You couldn't hear them but that was good and actually I did get a lot out of it.

GP: *What do you get out of making art?*
HH: There's an element of therapy about it. The great thing about doing art is that when I'm doing it, I'm completely in it and I'm not thinking about anything else, so I get that out. And at the end I get a thing. I don't sell them or I have no interest in exhibiting them.

Overleaf:
Soloman, 2020

Harry Hill

Beechwood and enamel paint
Courtesy of the artist

Add your own work here

Fantasy

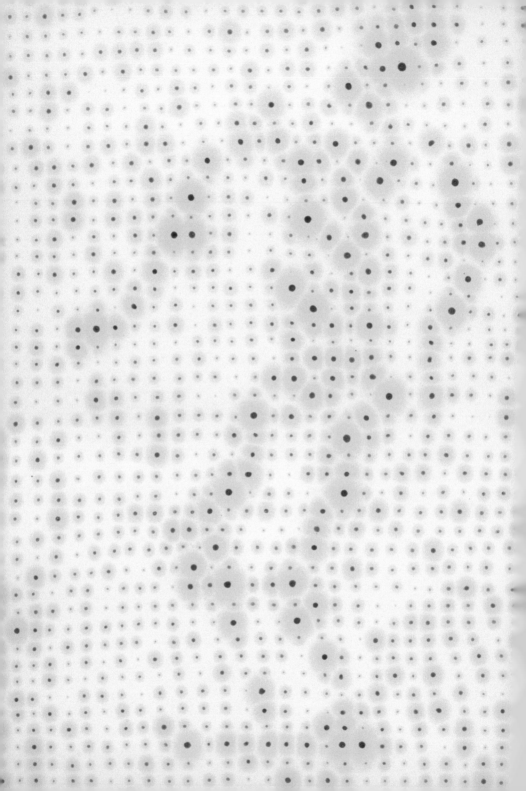

Antony Gormley

Artist

Antony Gormley: I always try to think of different ways of putting things together and different ways of exploring space itself. Three-dimensionality is a strange thing.

So, over recent days, this is what I've been doing: I have been quietly doing dots. I am making these drawings out of crude oil. I wanted to use a material that is the blood of the earth; that would somehow carry the feeling of geology, time, and substance. Every one of these points is distinct. I'm making something in time, that takes time to make and hopefully captures time. Here is this field of cells. They're also like frog spawn or eyeballs – or singularities.

Grayson Perry: How many people do you normally work with in your studio? It must be a long time since you've sat on your own in the studio.

AG: Usually 25 people work in the studio with me. I do work with a lot of people, but in the end, most things start in my little notebook that I keep in my back pocket, in brief notations: moments of extreme intimacy. Little ideas – a dream on one page and a drawing on the next – or just whole pages of drawings. This is where it all begins.

This time is luxury in a way. Here I am on my own. You have this opportunity now, I think, to dream and to expand your mind into areas that perhaps, in the busy time of fulfilling obligations, don't happen so naturally.

GP: What advice would you give to people if they wanted to start making sculptures at home?

AG: I would start carving soap. I've also been trying to get people to use barbecue sticks to make things. If you don't have barbecue sticks, try clay: go and dig some up or pick some up from the roadworks – there's a lot of clay under these islands. The kitchen table is a good studio!

Being an artist is an evolving process. There is no pinnacle, there is no achievement. It's a dialogue, it's an unfolding. Art is an open arena: an open country without borders. People can enter it as participants or as viewers, but better as both! Even a viewer is a participant, making some sense from something seen – but fundamentally, we're all makers.

Whether we are making our bed, making our breakfast, or making a bunch of flowers look good, we are all reacting to the visual stimuli in the world.

Previous:
Field
2020

Antony Gormley

Crude oil on paper
111.8 x 76.2cm

Raqib Shaw

Art:st

Grayson Perry: London-based artist Raqib Shaw fled strife-torn Kashmir as a teenager. Ever since then he's been creating extravagant fantasy landscapes filled with marvels and wonders. He took a break from painting and pruning his beloved bonsai trees to show Art Club *his studio.*

Raqib Shaw: I come from Kashmir and I had to leave in 1989. That's why lockdown is something that I'm quite used to because Kashmir was under lockdown for two years in the late 80s. It was actually then that I decided that I wanted to be an artist and that I would dedicate my life to making art, otherwise I would have been a salesman, working for my family's business.

I do always believe in that teeny bit of alchemy in art and transforming the base metal to gold and that element of magic, I think. It's quite important. I think we all need an element of magic in our lives. I put myself in my paintings because they are diaries of my experiences in life.

I'm with my dog, Mr C. You see that outside the balcony, it's absolute mayhem. There's war and there is destruction and yet the figure is concentrating on fireflies that are coming from the ground, which is all his imagination, and he's concentrating on beauty and positivity, as I think we all have to do that. Is it escapism? Of course it is escapism and I think that as we grow up, we totally forget about those things and we think about our mortgages.

You know, we will always have problems
but when you do art, it is that time that
you really forget about the problems
and you're really engaged in what you're
doing and the soul is free like a bird and
it flies in the sky. I think that is why art
is important. Don't you think?

Previous:
Ode to the Country without
a Post Office 2019
2020

Raqib Shaw

Acrylic liner and
enamel on birchwood
Courtesy of the artist and
White Cube

Greta
made

Thunberg
Covid
(FACT!)

Twins
2020

Laura Marrs

Mixed media, plaster of Paris,
canvas and acrylic
Courtesy of the artist

I don't really know now,
what I thought I knew then
2020

Leanne Jackson

Found imagery, digital
manipulation, Photoshop,
digital print
Courtesy of the artist

"When I was a kid, I was
fascinated with the idea that
when you suck up liquid in a
straw and then cover the end,
the water doesn't come out.
If it was possible on a tiny
tube, could you do it on a
big tube? Then if you could,
could you somehow get into
the top of the tube and swim
down, and then fall out of
the bottom? That's what I
thought of when I saw that."

Jessica Hynes

Celebrity
Pick

11 April, 2020, 19:03:04
2020

Seamus Killick

Photograph
Courtesy of the artist
Photography: Sarah Barnes

Led a merry dance
2020

Annabelle Tim Hogben

Oil on canvas
Courtesy of the artist

"I just really like her use of
paint. It felt like there was
something very expert about
her painting. I thought
you could spend some time
trying to work it out."

Jessica Hynes

Celebrity Pick

Covid–19
2020

Tom Rushmer

Digital giclée print
Courtesy of the artist

ComputerWorld
2020

Alex Robinson

Fimo clay
Courtesy of the artist

"Alex really nails what is
particularly great about
fantasy art. It took me
back to when I was young,
I escaped into a fantasy world
because I had control."

Grayson Perry

Grayson's Pick

Stranger Times I
2020

Carey Jane Still

Paper collage
Courtesy of the artist

Babyliss Burna
2020

Edmond Asher Brooks-
Beckham

Watercolour on paper
Courtesy of the artist

"They look like they've been
taking drugs for a very long
time, maybe a week. They
haven't left the room or
the house, which is very
lockdown-like. This is the
universe in his altered state
he finds himself in, and
actually that's not a clown,
that's his friend Rob coming
from the kitchen to ask if he
wants some toast. And he
thinks that's a real gun but
it's not, it's a hairdryer."

Jessica Hynes

Celebrity Pick

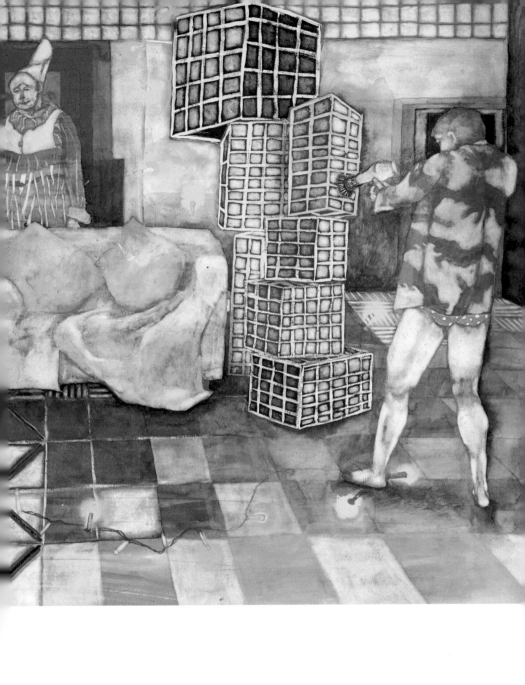

Needs a bit of updating
A surprise in the garden!
WOW
How can I
A Place in the Sun

A Place in the Sun
2020

Philippa Perry

Glazed ceramic
Courtesy of the artist

God in the Time of COVID–19
2020

Grayson Perry

Ceramic
Courtesy of the artist and
Victoria Miro

"Here we have the first scene,
which is Alan very upset
because Claire looks like
she's on death's door there.
Look, she's dropped her
Louis Vuitton handbag.
She is symbolic of the
economy because she does
spend a lot of money and
also she parties a lot.
Alan's there mourning and
he's really, really upset."

Grayson Perry

Jessica Hynes

Making a Fantasy Lampshade with Jessica Hynes

Nesting Bird – Ship at Sea
2020

Jessica Hynes

Oak frame, tracing paper,
copper wire, sharpies, double
sided sellotape
Courtesy of the artist

Jessica Hynes: I've made a few lampshades in the past and the easiest way to do is like this. You take an existing lampshade, a plain one and then you simply paint on it. You can paint anything you want on it. For this lampshade I'm gonna use a wood frame and tracing paper. So, we're gonna start off with a frame that is gonna be like a pentagon and then in each panel I've got a bit of tracing paper that I am going to paint and fix. I looked up online how to create a repeating pattern.
So, what I'm doing here is I've started to trace over this drawing.

So, these are the panels and I've coloured them all in. This is the frame. I've got double-sided sticky tape on the edges of the wood, so I'm just looking forward to putting it altogether and turning the light on and seeing what happens. Thank you *Grayson's Art Club* for inviting me to do this. I've had a ball and I know I wouldn't have done it otherwise, and I've had a lot of fun. Ship at sea and then a nesting bird, and all the fantasies in-between. I love it. I'm just looking at my lampshade.

Don't make it too complicated. If you've got a shade that's already made, probably start off with one that isn't your favourite and then just have a little play. It makes the object lovelier than it was before, even if it's a bit shonky because there's so much that's the same – we all kind of go to the same places and buy our lamp shades. You know, felt tips are brilliant. You might have a doodle pattern that you're always doodling whatever it is and you just get a white lampshade and just start doodling and it'll look beautiful or not.

You'll like it. You'll find that lamp shade definitely hard to sell, probably.

Grayson Perry: Jessica, how are you doing in lockdown?
JH: I have three children so I'm trying to make sure everyone is eating healthily but at the same time isn't getting bored with the same vegetable. (Laughter). Is that actually the same parsnip? 'It's a different parsnip cooked in a different way.'

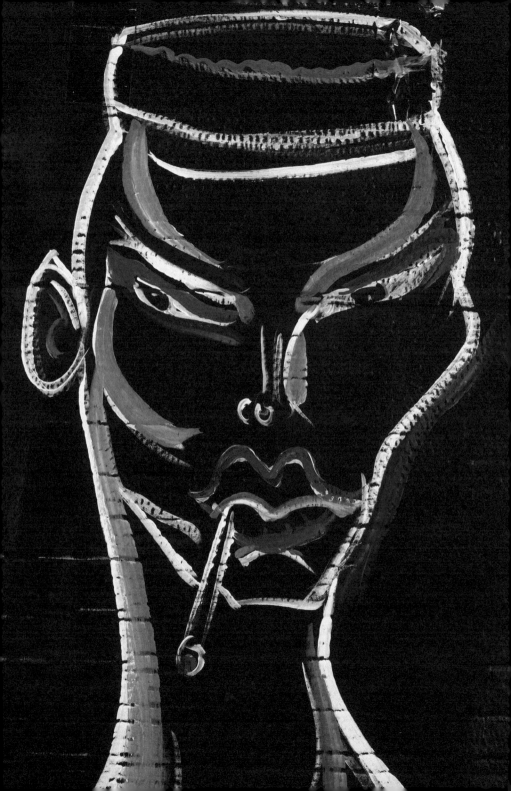

Noel Fielding

Fantasy Cocktail Party with Noel Fielding

Previous: Grace Jones, 2020

Noel Fielding

Acrylic and oil on card
Courtesy of the artist

Noel Fielding: I'm really excited. As you know, I'm very into fantasy but I was thinking, 'What's my lockdown fantasy?' I haven't been to a party for ages so like a sort of summer party in the garden, a cocktail party. So I'm working on the guest list now and obviously I can invite anyone in the universe. It's a fantasy party so it could be Jesus, it could be an African tree frog, it doesn't matter. I've gotta create those people and then position them round the garden and have a party with champagne, obviously. Maybe prosecco, I haven't got any champagne.

Let me introduce you to a couple of my guests. Grace Jones, the coolest of all my guests. She's used to partying at the Mudd Club and Studio 54. This is an art show so I've got two of my favourite artists. Andy Warhol, skinnier legs than me, and Jean Michel Basquiat, my favourite artist of all time. No offence Andy. Oh, we're friends anyway.

What would a party be without music? Nothing, that's what it would be. That's why I've got The Beatles in plate form. Paul, Ringo, John, George. I actually wanted The Stones but they were already booked up. I think Russell Brand was imagining them for his fantasy party. Over here is my guest of honour. You've gotta have a fantasy guest at a fantasy party, minotaur. He's had a little bit too much to drink, mythical creatures can't handle their beer.

The thing is about these guys, they don't need to do social distancing because they're not real. They say you can't have parties during lockdown but you can! But you just have to paint everyone yourself.

Grayson Perry: What a great party!
NF: I think some truth happened. I think all my frustration and all my anxiety came out. I just needed a release.

GP: *Well, you've gotta say that's one of the natures of fantasy. It's telling us what we want and need to happen and it's leaking out perhaps things that we don't wanna admit to.*
NF: Things we don't usually like to show that we keep concealed. Although I have done that quite a lot in public.

GP: *You've built a career on it.*
NF: Exactly. Growing up I liked Rudyard Kipling, *The Jungle Book* and I like Henri Rousseau, people who hadn't even been to the jungle and were imagining what the jungle might be like. And then, in the end, when I was making *The Mighty Boosh*, we would always be in the arctic tundra or we'd be in the jungle, or we'd be somewhere but most of these places we've

never been to, so they were made up of
our imagined versions which are always
all the best stuff from that place, you
know? Stylised version.

GP: *Noel, do you think in times of*
lockdown fantasy is more important
than ever?
NF: Absolutely because I think we're all
living in our minds. We're having a lot
of time to think. I think now everyone
is having to, sort of, have a look at
themselves and what they've been doing
and at their life, or what's important to
them, so I like that. I think actually that's
what it tapped into for me. Fantasy is
about using your imagination and once
you get all the clichés out the way, all of
the unicorns, all of that stuff, then it gets
interesting and you're sort of delving into
your subconscious or something. I think
you have to put yourself into a bubble, a
place where you can play all the time, so
you have to keep real life a little bit at bay.
You have to keep out council tax bills and
adverts, and all of this stuff that if you can
keep that all at bay and create a little cave,
a fantasy cave like your studio, or like I
do, then when you're in there, it triggers
something in your brain and then you feel
free enough to play. And that's when all
the good stuff comes out, I think.

Jean-Michel Basquiat
2020

Noel Fielding

Acrylic and oil on card
Courtesy of the artist

My Fantasy...

View

W

From my

indow

Thank God For Immigrants

Jeremy Deller

Artist

Jeremy Deller: In 1993 I did an exhibition in my parent's house when they went on holiday and I called it *Open Bedroom*. And then the show really went all over the house, so I took down the art that they'd bought and I put up my own work. They didn't find out about it for years 'cause I thought they'd be angry that I'd done it.

One of the works was a quote from *Waterloo Sunset*, 'every day I look at the world from my window'.

Before the lockdown, I bought thirteen notebooks because I was so scared that I'd run out, so I panicked and I'm just looking back at what I did at the beginning. I was thinking about if there's gonna be some kind of huge celebration at the end of this and some national moment of memorial or celebration at the end of the pandemic. There could be people dressing up as the virus and then people dressing up as syringes and they attack the virus or chase it and it's, sort of, funny almost. I also made a poster to go in the windows of people's houses and flats, *Thank God for Immigrants*. I thought it was good to use not only 'immigrant' but also 'God' in the same sentence.

I thought it was important to do that – two very contentious, loaded words and I made it as a poster that people could put in their windows and it could be seen from the streets. So much art now that we see is things that people put up in their windows, mainly children. So, streets have become forms of galleries in a way where people are showing you what they think about the NHS or what's going on, a bit like a bumper sticker on a car.

In 1997, I got a brass band to play acid house music, which on its surface I suppose sounds like a bit of a joke. But really I was trying to get to make a work of art in a way really that

explained British history in the 20th Century through music. The relationship between brass bands and acid house was going from being an industrial society to a post-industrial society. Acid brass was the first time I'd worked with the public really. It really taught me so much in the sense that I realised the public were up for doing stuff. The public aren't really afraid of art and artists.

Some of the first works I made were posters and I had a lot of enjoyment putting them up in the street or in buildings and just letting them live there and see how long they stayed up. It's something I've always been interested in putting work up in public and just seeing what the reaction is to it. That's never left me. In a way it's a great way to react to a situation as well. For me, it's always a thrill to see something that I've done put up in the street. That's a big compliment, maybe even more so than having something put up in an art gallery.

Grayson Perry: Welcome to Art Club, Jeremy. The theme is the view from your window.
JD: One of the things I've really enjoyed is walking down streets and seeing what people have put up in their windows

Previous:
Thank God for Immigrants
2020

Jeremy Deller and
Fraser Muggeridge

Limited edition print to raise
funds for Refugee Action and
The Trussel Trust
Courtesy of the artists

and it's developing, isn't it? You know, it's children's things but then people put up phrases. Someone's put up a sort of shop dummy near us and every day it's different what he or she's done and written things on the window and so on, put up posters. So, that's been something I actually quite enjoyed, people using that and it's become a bit more sophisticated. I mean, this whole thing about the eight o'clock on the Thursdays, you know, that's a big piece of performance, isn't it? It's a national performance.

GP: *Yeah, like it's something you might have organised.*
JD: Well, kind of. Yes, it's interesting, isn't it, the way it's happened and the way it's proliferated and maybe the meaning of it will change over time. It is support definitely for the NHS, which is absolutely real and genuine but also there might be, it might be tinged with frustration and anger and it'll be interesting to see where that goes.

GP: *What do you think though all of what's happening at the moment is telling us about the state of the nation?*
JD: Well, that's a big question for me.

GP: *I think you're the ideal artist to ask that question to, Jeremy.*
JD: Oh, no. Maybe. I wasn't expecting that one. I'm gonna be more optimistic about Britain. This is literally a once in a century opportunity to reorientate society after the Second World War. The greatest memorial to the Second World War is the NHS. It's not like a war memorial, it's actually that institution and I think we need to work out what the institution or what the direction will be after this because we can't carry on as normal.

I

Blame

SG!

View from My Window
2020

Julia Gardner

Oil on canvas
Courtesy of the artist

"I think there's quite a lot
going on. There's a face
over to the left, a green
lady looking straight at us,
and the perspective is non-
existent which I really like.
The blackbird in the middle
of the lawn would probably
be about 5ft long!"

Jim Moir

Celebrity Pick

So Near Yet So Far
2020

Clare Wilks

Coloured inks on paper
Courtesy of the artist

Window with a Fresh View
2020

Vinny Montag and
Kimvi Nguyen

Fridge, fabric, food and drink
Courtesy of the artist

Untitled
2020

Freya Moffat

Giclée print
Courtesy of the artist

"I couldn't work this one
out at first which made me
intrigued and look closer,
which is always a good thing.
Is it a papier-mâché person
who looks a bit like an elf?"

Jim Moir

Celebrity
Pick

enjoying the view from
my window,
Tuesday 05 May 2020, 6:47 a.m
2020

Andrew Brownsell

Digital photo
Courtesy of the artist

My view from my window,
2020

Emma Major

Pen on paper
Courtesy of the artist

View From Your Window

My view?
Blurry glimpses in darkness
Memory clarifies
Digital amplifies
Senses fill the void
What do you see?

Out of my window
2020

David Stuart Tomlinson

Acrylic on board
Courtesy of the artist

"I love it. I really, really like
it. It looks like a theme park
that's just been dropped onto
the middle of the lawn."

Jim Moir

Celebrity Pick

The view from my window,
starring my beautiful
cat Leon
2020

Bethany Kelly

Print and collage
Courtesy of the artist

Nuts About Life
2020

Clare Ward

Watercolour on paper
Courtesy of the artist

"It's the emptyness on it
I like, and then of course
you've got 'Nuts About
Life' there and every bit
of surface satisfies me.
It hasn't got any weak

spots on it. The trees, the
pavement, the bins, the car,
everything is perfect.
I absolutely adore it."

Grayson Perry

House Planter
2020

Grayson Perry

C–type print
Courtesy of the artist
and Victoria Miro

"Oh, inside we've got
wallpaper still left in, just a
strip of it. Oh it's beautiful.
I absolutely love it and it's
so nice 'cause it's our house."

Philippa Perry

Jim Moir aka Vic Reeves

Painting Garden Birds with Jim Moir

Previous: Bearded Tit, 2020

Jim Moir

Oil on canvas
Courtesy of the artist

Jim Moir: I sit here looking at my bird station quite a lot. A bit more now in lockdown but what I really like is I've got a myriad of seeds and I can see the action of the birds. You just think birds are nice, kind of, fluffy. 'Oh, aren't they nice? They're pretty, aren't they?' But really when you look at them a bit longer, you'll find out that they're a very violent species. The robin, which is Britain's national bird, is probably one of the most violent gangsters in the world.

You can watch the whole thing like a Tarantino style soap opera. You can see it all unfold, the violence, the occasional love and whilst I'm looking at the birds, I play my organ.

What I'm gonna do is use oil sticks in really primary colours. The hierarchy of the tits is you've got the great tit, which is in charge, and then that'll see off a blue tit, which is a bit smaller and then a blue tit will see off maybe two or three long-tailed tits. They live alongside the coal tit quite nicely. There are other tits that I haven't seen like crested tits or a tell-tale-tit. Now, that will be a thing.

A tell-tale-tit which could go and have a look through people's windows and then come back and then maybe give me post-it notes. Tiny ones the size of, like, miniature stamps that elves might have with information about what other people are doing in the area.

Right, so I'm gonna get on now and do these birds. The good thing about these oils is they really hold their colour against a darker colour. You don't get too much bleed or mess. Look at that, it is like butter. It's so soft. Actually you just wanna lick it. Don't, you'd probably die!

I love primary colours as well and especially in these salty times, it's good to see bright colours, bright primary colours because it cheers people up.

Well, here we are, here I am at the end of a morning's work. It's one o'clock now. I started work at 8:00am on this one here, the gold crest, which I'm kind of alright with. Then I moved onto the waxwing. Then I moved onto Reggae superstars. We've got Gregory Isaacs, the cool ruler, the king of lover's rock and there is Big Youth who I used to listen to a lot when I was a youth.

Over there we've got the bearded tit. Inside of the greenhouse we've got the Dartford warbler, which is a very tiny bird. I've never actually seen one but I hope to. Finally what's this? This is a bee eater, so there we are. That is my exhibition in this gallery which is locally known as 'the greenhouse'.

Do the
social

distancing

Dance!

Grayson Perry: *Welcome to* Art Club
Jim. You went to art school, what's your
relationship to art now?
JM: Well that's what it's always been.
I ended up doing comedy because I
thought I was doing a performance piece
and people thought it was hilarious so I
carried on, but art painting has been my
main job every day really and it's like the
TV stuff, sort of, in between.

GP: So, if you were to give one tip to the
people of the world to start making art
what would you say? Where would you
say to start?
JM: I think people are clearing out rubbish,
aren't they? Out of their garages and that.
There's a lot of cardboard lying about. You
don't need to get canvasses now. Get your
cardboard and stick things on it and draw
on it, and use the stuff in your house.

your

made

work

here

Home

ACCEPT YOUR PORRIDGE

YOU CANNOT CHANGE IT

David Shrigley

Artist

David Shrigley: I am currently living in Devon where I'm in lockdown. I'm gonna show you some drawings that I've made.

These seem to be about the situation we're in to some extent. 'Accept your porridge, you cannot change it'. 'We shall be good friends, you and I and we shall spend much time together'. Over the years I've become sort of the go-to guy in the world of fine art who makes funny drawings. 'We wash but why?' I'm lucky because I can entertain myself.

I have a certain amount of drawings that I have to do in a day. I just focus on making that number of drawings. I think at the beginning of my professional career I just shied away a little bit from the fact that my work's funny. I kind of wanted it to be poetic or profound in some way, whereas now I think that I kind of embrace the comedy of it. I think that comedy is something, it's a gift, to be able to laugh.

I think the central problem being an artist is the starting point. Once you've got a starting point then the artwork makes itself. It's the starting point that's hard, so for me just having a set number of drawings to make in a day is enough of a starting point. I just tell myself it doesn't matter what your drawings are like because I discard a lot anyway. As long as they're finished then my work is done.

Previous:
Untitled
2020

David Shrigley

Ink on paper
Courtesy of the artist
and Stephen Friedman
Gallery, London

1m +

My arse!

Barbie in Lockdown
2020

Anita Kapila

Cardboard, wool, polyester,
plastic, metal, paper, nylon
Courtesy of the artist

How many kids in lockdown?
2020

Sue Dibben

Collage
Courtesy of the artist

"I thought it stood out
because it is obviously from
somebody who really knows
what they're doing, it's the
detail. It's one of those pieces
of work that you can actually
stand in front of and see
more and more the longer
you look at it. It's great."

Jenny Eclair

Celebrity
Pick

Fag On
2020

Janine Chisholm Sullivan

Giclée print from digital
drawing on Procreate
Courtesy of the artist

"It's like 'You better eat this
Sunday lunch, I've slaved over
a hot stove for you', and the
grandpa is going 'Yeah, I'll
break ya kneecaps if you don't
eat it'. I like it very much."

Jenny Eclair

Grayson's Pick

Home
2020

Anna Christophersen

Polymer clay sculptures and
photography with digital
manipulation
Courtesy of the artist

"I like the fact it's a slightly
alien landscape, which I
think lockdown has been.
And although homes are
sweet and familiar, they're
very distant from each other."

Jenny Eclair

Celebrity
Pick

Home is where you park it
2020

Jenny Brennan

Poster paints on paper
Courtesy of the artist

At home with my cats
2020

Ania Newland

Acrylic on canvas
Courtesy of the artist

"This for me really sums up a
lot about lockdown. Also the
style is very current I think.
It has a kind of kooky, slightly
kitsch millennial vibe about
it, which I like very much."

Grayson Perry

Grayson's Pick

Loafing in the living room
2020

Anthony King

Collage, mixed media
Courtesy of the artist

"It's just a very gentle rather
sweet domestic scene and it's
just pleasing and easy to live
with, and I liked it."

Jenny Eclair

Celebrity Pick

Home is where the (he)art is
2020

Simran and Mandish Khebbal

Collage
Courtesy of the artists

"I think it tells us something
very fundamental about home.
In that, it's where your heart is.
It's where you carry your love."

Grayson Perry

Grayson's Pick

The Gay Commune
2020

Philippa Perry

Glazed ceramic
Courtesy of the artist

Next:
Tea Towel
2020

Grayson Perry

Tea towel (cotton twill
Courtesy of the artist and
Victoria Miro

"I'm starting a supermarket
chain called 'Someone'
and it'll have someone on
every packet. So you know
someone out there, who's
really important, packaged
or made it."

Grayson Perry

Jenny Eclair

Painting Home with Jenny Eclair

Previous: Corner of my sitting room, 2020

Jenny Eclair

Black paper and oil pastel crayon.
Courtesy of the artist

Jenny Eclair: Welcome to my studio, AKA the kitchen table. I don't think you should have a studio unless you can sell your work and I don't. These are my favourite things which I use, I call them wax crayons. They obviously aren't really wax crayons. They're oil pastels and these, can I just say, these smell really good too.

I'm gonna leave my kitchen studio and have a mooch around the house and see if I can find any inspiration of Grayson's theme this week, which is home. There's something about this pot here that is actually talking to me rather because I do spend a lot of time sitting on my bum and this looks like something I could tackle. In fact, I think I'm gonna set up in this corner here and try and capture this. Wish me luck. The good thing about wax crayons is that they're very, very forgiving. Just rough, rough, rough, rough, rough for now.

The thing is, it's not brain surgery. If it goes wrong, it's not gonna kill anybody. It'll just destroy my confidence. It doesn't matter. It doesn't have to be perfect, don't be silly. As long as you don't cry, Jenny. That's the most important thing. Do not break down over this, okay everybody? That's the rule.

We built this house. I say 'we' built this house. I did nothing. I didn't lift a finger. My partner was trained as an artist. I do live with somebody who's very entrenched in the art world.

So, there she is. There's my picture of home.

Grayson Perry: How have you found your attitude to your home changing during this period?
JE: I love my home and I wouldn't moan for a second but between you and me, I'm a bit sick of it, do you know what I mean? There are moments when I just think, 'I'd really like to drink a cup of coffee out of a mug I don't own.' I'd even like to use a pan that's not mine. Familiarity is leading to a bit of contempt, even though home for me is a huge sanctuary and whenever I write books, houses are where I start.

GP: I hear you're making a painting every day?
JE: Every day. There's no quality control but it is regular and I think that I'm getting better at drawing, a bit.

GP: Is having Jeff [Jenny's partner] the designer, artist in the home, is that part of your kind of confidence issues with your art do you think?
JE: No, no, no but he won't help me. He sometimes goes, 'Oh, just think about

Go to work

DON'T

GO TO

WORK !

your perspective.' When he was young, I used to call him the Style Nazi. When I moved in on him, it was like The Great Escape in reverse. He didn't want me to move in and I was desperate and I'd just bring things over from my flat and he had no furniture at all. He just had one easy chair and then in a sitting room there was a big pebble.

He's been really encouraging with my art. He's been buying me bigger and bigger pads of black paper. I think he sort of wants me to get bigger.

That'll teach him.

Kevin McCloud

Making Home with Kevin McCloud

Previous: Happiness Bungalow, 2020

Kevin McCloud

Cardboard and cork sculpture
Courtesy of the artist

Kevin McCloud: The miniature world I want to construct is one that I've never done before, which is a sort of mind palace. It isn't a model of a real place, it's a model of a fictitious building and one I would probably never ever build.

This is like a simple schematic version of the medieval cloister. The idea of the cloister is very important for me – it's a safe space. I like the idea it's COVID-19 that we, kind of, create and try to create even in imaginary spaces in our heads, somewhere safe that we can retreat to.

So, I'm making my little model out of packing cardboard. It's like a cardboard box and here are three pieces of card glued together and here is a facing of cork, as you can see. It just gives it a real cool look and you could use all kinds of things for model making. I mean, you could just cover that with cork, a sheet like that would look amazing and I'm gonna experiment with some other stuff anyway, depending on what's in the bin.

Grayson, it is with some trepidation that I reveal to you the workings of my mind.

So, I built this, sort of, almost medieval looking cloister in the middle of it. To the south is the Jam Tent because that embodies two great loves of my life, that's music and making jam. That is a greenhouse with a very large tomato in it. I like growing veg. I have an allotment and the tomato is the tomato of my dreams. This building is called The Tower of Love and in it you can just see there is the heart of happiness.

Then finally a little balloon of imagination, escape and adventure and the idea of being able to take flight seems to be woven into this silly thing. I realise now I could have made a collage, which would have taken a tenth of the time and be just as good, if not better, but there you go. I didn't.

Grayson Perry: What practical tips would you give to people for improving their home to make them more creative and delightful, and to also have a positive effect on them?

KMC: There's a terrible pressure on all of us, to conform and I say 'has been' because I think COVID has changed this. I think we're in a world where it was all about having the same car, the same kind of interior, the same items, the same pieces of furniture as our neighbours and friends. We're all in this kind of club of brands together, whereas getting out that old record player or the poster we had when we were student or that bit of furniture that Gran gave us, or the

painting that belonged to Mum but
which you didn't really think fitted with
your furniture but actually has a huge
sentimental and important, personal
value. That stuff is really interesting.

GP: And what has lockdown taught you
about the kind of idea of home?
KMC: You know, I just think it happens
on Thursday evening when people come
out to the street and they clap. They're
extending the physical boundaries of
their home from the building out into
the street because they're sharing within
the community that thing and it's really
powerful and healthy for communities,
for streets, to do that, to keep pushing
those boundaries.
    We've had to adjust, haven't we,
to shrinking it back and therefore,
I suppose, in looking at certainly a
blank wall, focusing on it and thinking,
'Well, how can I make this richer?'

Banana Bread
coming out
of every
orifice!

Add
your
own
work
here

And
here

Bri

rain

HERD IMMUNITY

OH, grant me this boon that I may not hesitate from performing good actions. I may not fear the enemy, when I go to fight and assuredly I become victorious. And when my mortal life comes to an end, may I die fighting courageously on the battlefield.

(Sri Guru Gobind Singh Ji)

HEED THE WARNINGS • PROVIDE PPE • SAVE LIVES

STAY ALERT • IGNORE THE BS • STAY ALIVE

You can't clap away the surcharge increase

LIVERPOOL FC V. ATLETICO MADRID

Brexit: Anti-immigrant prejudice major factor in deciding vote, study finds (Ian Johnston - Independent, 22 June 2017)

"In it Together?"

CARE HOME workers like 'lambs to the slaughter' without proper access to PPE. (ITV News, 4 May, 2020)

THE NHS SAVED BORIS. NOW GIVE US A PAYRISE!

BRITAIN MISSED three opportunities to be part of an EU scheme to bulk-buy masks, gowns and gloves. (Daniel Boffey and Robert Booth - The Guardian, 13th April 2020)

FRONTLINE NHS staff have resorted to buying masks at DIY stores... ...doctors have criticised the quality and quantity of [Government] supplies.

BAME groups face two to three times higher risk of death from COVID-19 (Nick Bostock - GP online, 7 may 2020). NHS 'needs BAME staff to run' (Shailesh Solanki - Eastern Eye, 8 May 2020)

GROWING ALARM AMONG SCIENTISTS appears not to have been heard or heeded by policy-makers. The failure to obtain large amounts of testing equipment - was another big error of judgement....Considerable capacity of Britain's private laboratories to mass-produce tests was not harnessed during those crucial weeks of February. (Insight team - The Sunday Times, 19 April 2020)

PUBLIC sector pay freeze after covid-19 would 'outrage' nurses and patients. (Rebecca Gilroy - Nursing Times, 14 May 2020)

The Singh Twins

Artists

Grayson Perry: The Singh twins are two Wirral based artists I really admire. They combine traditions from both Eastern and Western art to make provocative and sharply political work. They showed Art Club how they've been producing their own very personal take on this extraordinary moment in our history.

Singh Twins: This is our latest work, it is a piece which responds to the COVID situation.

Stylistically the artwork's eclectic. It's a combination of hand painting together with modern digital technologies, so some of the artwork has actually been created using computer tools, some has been created using scanned imagery and some other details are actually all hand painted. It's all come together within the computer, so the final piece actually only exists as a digital image.

So, this is one of the painted elements of the COVID artwork which was originally drawn onto this board and then hand painted, then the image was scanned into the computer. We're going to overlay it with further details, so here's some COVID viruses which have been created in the computer by hand using digital tools. We're going to reduce that and then drag it across to the final COVID artwork on the left of the screen here.

Overall the artwork is a tribute to the NHS and other healthcare workers. The NHS is represented by an Asian nurse who's riding a horse and she's fighting the

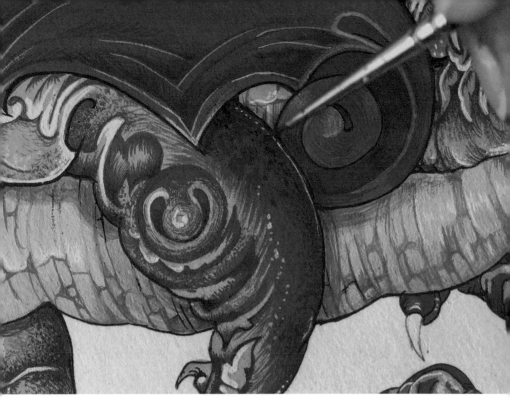

COVID dragon, if you like, but she's being held back by Boris Johnson who's pulling on the horse's reins and at the same time stabbing her in the back.

The central figures are actually a reinterpretation of the Christian figure of Saint George slaying the dragon, really reflecting this whole idea of how immigrant communities or communities that are seen as other have left their imprint on British society. Saint George, who's the patron saint of England, in actual fact, was Turkish in origin.

You know, saints were ordinary people who did extraordinary things and in the same way the NHS workers are extraordinary people, putting their lives on the line for the benefit of the rest of us.

Previous:
NHS v COVID: fighting
on Two Fronts
2020

The Singh Twins

Lightbox
Courtesy of the artists

*GP: Your fabulous artwork, it could not
be more of the moment and beautiful.
I am in awe of your skills.*
ST: Oh, thank you. Well, the feeling
is mutual, really.

*GP: And I believe that there is a sort
of personal motivation in this artwork
you have made.*
ST: Yeah, very sadly we lost a friend,
who was a national health worker, to the
COVID virus and although we'd been
thinking about tackling this subject,
watching it avidly over the past few months,
I think it was that event that basically
made us do it sooner rather than later.
      Certainly out of anger I
think more than anything else. The
unnecessary loss of a friend and how
that also impacted in terms of the
universal story of the loss of many lives,
particularly amongst the NHS workers.
So, that was one of the main motivations
behind this particular piece.

*GP: Has the crisis changed your idea
about Britain and British identity at all?*
ST: Not really but I think it's confirmed
the fact that the so-called ethnic minority
communities have a very valid place to
play within our society and always have
had. I'm hoping that one of the positive
things that comes out of this crisis is that
those people that perhaps may not be on
the same page in terms of that particular
line of thinking, will think again about all
those people who may not be perceived
to be British or English but in actual
fact, are as much a part of our society
as anybody else.

Martin Parr

Artist

Grayson Perry: All his working life the photographer Martin Parr has been holding up a mirror to the British. For me no other artist so perfectly captures our rituals and our foibles. He's made a film for Art Club *about how he's been photographing Britain during lockdown.*

Martin Parr: One of the things we do very well is queue. We're very efficient at it and low and behold anyone who tries to push in, they'll be given short shrift. Often, of course, these are in the pre-pandemic time, everyone was very close together. Now we have a different type of queue where everyone's spaced out, so I'm now adopting my pictures to show the new COVID-19 queue and how it looks. Because people are so far distanced now you have to look for something else to bring all these pictures together, so either you go at a slight angle to the queue and you hope for a very plain background which will help to isolate people. I've had to adapt as we go along because you never know exactly when a queue is gonna take place.

GP: The theme is Britishness. You've given us some choice photographs from your back catalogue here. Can you take me through these images and tell me what you think they tell us about Britishness? Starting with St George's Day, West Bromwich.
MP: Yeah, so the biggest St George's Day parade is in West Brom and it's quite an event. It's interesting that most people don't know when St George's Day is, you know? But here it's a massive thing

and, of course, this is when people get their English flags out. You can see here the bulldog dressed accordingly and the parade, well, it must be like a mile long. It's a huge event and it's unique to the Black Country. It's interesting that all the other countries, you know, Scotland, Wales, any other country in Europe, have a national day while us, we still don't have it as a bank holiday. So it's fascinating how it's almost like it comes from underneath and becomes very important to the people in that particular locality.

GP: The next image I've got here is of the Iftar Festival in Bristol.
MP: This is in St Mark's Road and it's a fantastic event. So, this is to celebrate the end of Ramadan and the whole Muslim community invite anyone who wants to come, to come to this street, sit in the middle of it and you're fed a meal when the sun goes down. It's a very strong event and it is, for me, for me, one of the most moving things that I've seen. There must be 1,000 people sat in the street all eating this food together, whether you're Muslim or not, everyone is welcome.

GP: And my last image here is Princess Café Scarborough, 1988.
MP: In fact I went there about two years ago and that same painting of the boat is still on the wall and it still looks like that, and it's one of those classic scenes that is so quintessentially British that it almost makes me cry when I look at it. I'm not actually allowed at the moment to go into such an establishment and I can't wait to get back in.

GP: Aww, that is sweet. I understand what you mean. So, what do you think are the quintessential qualities of Britishness?
MP: I have this quite complex relationship to my own country, you know. I sort of love it and hate it at the same time and that is why photographing it is where I can actually manifest this seeming contradiction and ambiguity into the pictures where there are some things that are reassuring and some things which are annoying. You know, how do you combine those two things? That's why I can articulate it much better as a photographer and that's how I can try and produce images where that sort of tension is manifest.

GP: I think you've put your finger on something there that I've been trying to articulate, which is my feelings about Britain. I'm like you, I'm conflicted but maybe that is Britishness. We all have that love hate thing going on.
MP: Exactly, yeah. How to articulate that is quite difficult and the ultimate challenge but one that one can never fully finish. That's why I continue doing this, it's almost like a calling that I have to photograph this country. It's not just a task, it's a calling.

GP: Thank you, Martin. Speaking with Martin there, almost, in a flash of neon, I saw Britishness in front of me and I think the thing we've got to come round to is half of the country disagree with you and maybe you wouldn't wanna be next to them in a queue but that's the country we're in and we've gotta get used to that idea, you know? And, maybe we'll come round to love each other a bit more.

Previous: Sainsbury's queue during the coronavirus outbreak, Bedminster, Bristol 2020

Martin Parr

Photographic prints
Courtesy of the artist

The Way Ahead
2020

Jasmine Horn

Acrylic on paper
Courtesy of the artist

"It gave me goose bumps
actually when I first saw
that and it's wistful that you
can't see who those people
are and they're looking out
at whatever, the future but,
again, possibilities"

Liza Tarbuck

Celebrity Pick

Thursday, 8pm
2020

Jacqueline Taylor

Oil on canvas
Courtesy of the artist

"I saw that and I thought,
'in ten years time if that was
seen anywhere, it would
take us back to right now.
So, I think it's very sure
of itself and it's sure of it's
place in history."

Liza Tarbuck

Celebrity
Pick

Britain, The Queen and me
2020

Georgia Rusch

Acrylic inks and pen on paper
Courtesy of the artist

Britain

the Queen and me

Overleaf:
A British-ish Flag
2020

Olivia Winteringham

Coloured felt, sequins, tassel
fringe, cotton
Courtesy of the artist

It's not just time that heals
2020

Sue and Adrian Dent

Ceramic, terracotta with slip
decoration and gold coloured
resin filler
Courtesy of the artists

"A new flag for new times.
We don't need to hark back
anymore, we need to look
forward. I liked it's Peter
Blake-iness. I'm an absolute
swine for a bit of neon pink."

Liza Tarbuck

"A mystifying object, which
I am super intrigued by.
It looks a bit like chain mail,
it looks like a mask."

Grayson Perry

Celebrity
Pick

Grayson's
Pick

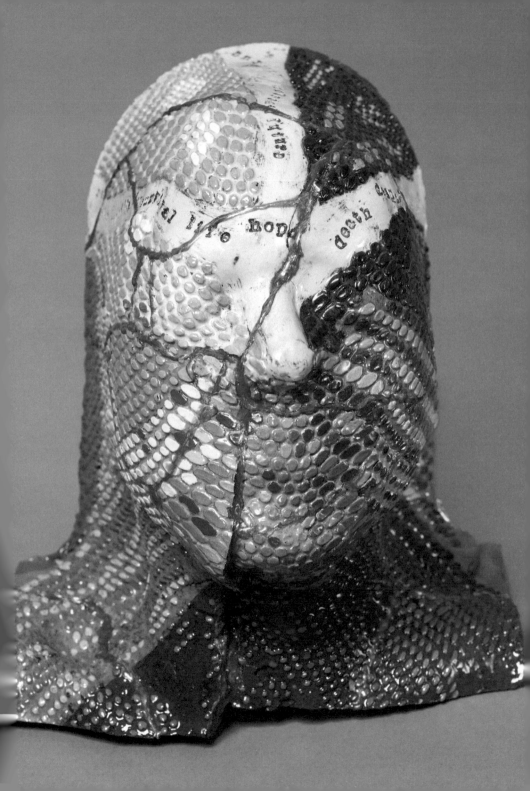

The Judgement
2020

Lana Turner

Mixed media, paper, pen
Courtesy of the artist

L. Turner

Greetings from
Lockdown London
2020

Yui Archer

Photograph, card, paper
Courtesy of the artist

"It's a really nice photograph.
In one image we have 'don't
go here' tape, but the tape
has been moved. There's the
idea that, did someone sit on
this bench? Which is very
English, I've got to say."

Grayson Perry

Grayson's
Pick

reetings from

LONDON

ENG.

Britain
2020

Philippa Perry

Glazed ceramics
Courtesy of the artist

I LOVE MY HOME AND I WOULDN'T
BIT SICK OF IT, D'YOU KNOW WHA
NOT BEING ABLE TO HUG THEM
VEN'T BEEN WASHED BECAUSE SH
TING THERE NEXT TO HER NHS
OF SHRINKING. THERE SEEMS
INE HARD. SHE'S GOT STRIPY
WE SHALL SPEND MUCH TIME
CHANGE IT. I'D REALLY LIK
DON'T OWN. A BARBIE IN A
THING.
I AM DISSATISFIED WITH
FEELS ENDLESS. WILL THE
LECTED IN MY FACE? A LITTL
A LITTLE BIT FRIGHTENED
WE ARE NOT OSTRICHES WE
CING UP TO THE SITUATION
ALLY REALLY STRANGE. FO
CATS ARE INCREDIBLY HAPP
WATCHING BOX SETS ON
NEXT YEAR, WHO KNOWS
NONE OF THEM

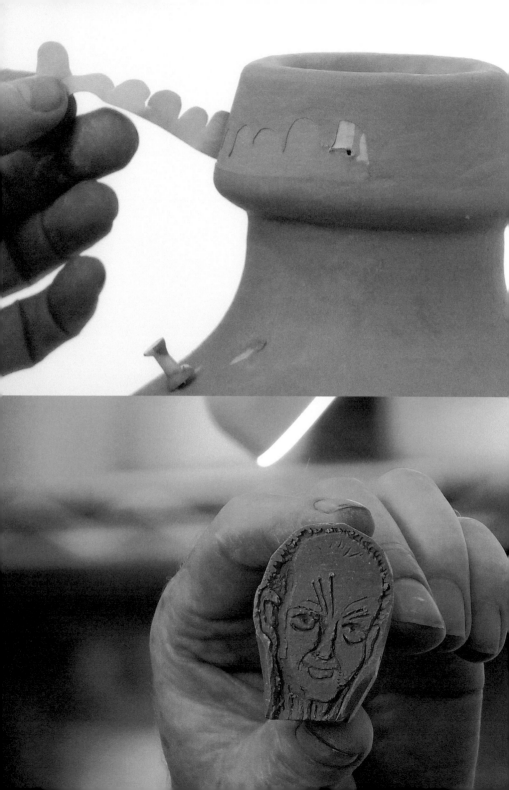

We Shall Catch it on
the Beaches
2020

Grayson Perry

Ceramic
Courtesy of the artist
and Victoria Miro

"Well, that is Britain. If
we are world leading in
anything, it's hypocrisy."

Grayson and Philippa Perry

Liza Tarbuck

Crafting Britain with Liza Tarbuck

Ginger McGinge, 2020
Liza Tarbuck

Mixed media, inc. wooden
box, mosaic, paint and fabric
Courtesy of the artist

Liza Tarbuck: Welcome to my craft room. I've come upstairs to have a good route around my cloth bags because I quite like a bit of patchy sewing. So I made a copy of the map but mine looks like an old lady. And then I lay my fabric out, put that on top and cut it, obviously, and I kind of wanted to see whether as a bit of fabric it looked more like a butterfly but it's a bit ink blotty, isn't it? I just thought I better introduce you to my dog, Mr Ringo S Tarbuck.

When I cut the map out it was a little bit more awkward than I thought and I, kind of, got rid of, err, the Sussex area. I'm at a good stage. There's me map. I found a good box and now I need to find a way of suspending it in there, because we're in a state of suspension.

Here's my box – I painted it inside and out. This is a panel I made years ago for my old kitchen. If you are doing this obviously wearing glasses is essential. I've really annoyed Ringo this week, I don't know what I've done except feed him and be his slave. That man next door has been sanding his garden for two-and-a-half months. Four-and-a-half hours he did one Sunday. Imagine my joy. Yeah, I had a word. Also, just to let you know I've buggered the 'n' up on the artwork.

There's Dan Pora's box. It's been opened, let's have a look at it. If you look inside we've got the pools of reflection and the mosaic helps for that sort of refracted different angle of yourself. It doesn't have to be one big thing, it's lots of little things and there's the British Isles. Apologies to certain islands hanging on by a thread allegedly but looking really rather firm. I've added the ley lines to represent the invisible threat of the virus but, in actual fact, the invisible is a beautiful place that we inhabit, whether it be earth energy and ley lines or integrity and faith. I'm so deep.

Now, if you're looking at yourself you might be, because of all the different facets, you might be seeing yourself in ways for the first time. I have actually lost the Orkneys for now. I'll put them back in but I really enjoyed doing this and it's on a frame so that I could have the British Isles hanging by a thread but it's not, it's really quite firm.

Grayson Perry: I believe my wife is the Scrabble fanatic and she spotted Dan Pora was an anagram of 'Pandora'. Is that right?
LT: Thanks, Philippa.

GP: What do you think your artwork is saying about Britain now?

Covid
Britain

LT: It's about possibility for going forward
and if it's not time for change now,
when will it be?

GP: Yes, that's exactly it. If now is not the
time, how desperate do we have to be?
LT: Yeah, exactly.

GP: How are you feeling about Britain?
LT: I was very interested in all the war
time parlance that started quite early on.

GP: Totally agree with you.
LT: You could see the thinking of, like,
'Quick, make him more like Churchill.'
          But it was in that beginning
of lockdown, where politicians weren't
aware of their backgrounds. So they'd be
Zooming and trying to get their point
across and you're like, 'Oh, look at that
landscape.' So they were letting the
human sides of themselves show, which
was a really good thing. But then they
added a line of deception, of show biz,
which of course, as it's gone on,, we've
all got used to – you know, bad roots,
no makeup, not necessarily even washing.

GP: I think you make an interesting point
there in that the audience are not daft,
they can smell being spun to a mile away.
LT: It's exactly that. It's a very intimate
process, as a consequence of that stop it.
You've got an opportunity just to stop it.

work

here

here

work

Grayson Perry

A lan
Measles

Protective
Spirit

Grayson Perry: One constant throughout this series has been Alan Measles, my personal deity. He's my childhood teddy bear named after the disease I had when I was about three. So he's the perfect candidate for a protective spirit in the middle of a pandemic. As soon as this crisis started to happen, I thought as my metaphor for God, he would have to play a part in some way. So, I've made this sculpture of him.

I wanted him to look like he's got antenna because one of my inspirations for this are the sculptures of an outsider artist called Emery Blagden and he made these healing machines. They were imaginary electromagnetic force field generators that would have a positive effect on health. So there's an element of this sculpture that Alan is a great big aerial for some kind of psycho power. So, eventually you'll have a kind of halo of rusty aerials. I found this lovely sheet of brass on the beach and it's all beautifully corroded and it's nice to work, and I've made a pair of little doors out of that to go on the front of the shrine. Behind the doors this should be the kind of Holy Grail, if you like, and so maybe something like the symbolic carrier of the cure. Probably about 90% bleach, and about 10% bullshit in there.

This sculpture of him is pretty well done. He's been through a bit of a transformation, he looks about 100 years older than he was, because I threw him in the sea for a century basically and he's got all this algae growing on him. 'Cause he's made of all different stuff, it's a way of me bringing him altogether and making him look like he's been lying on a beach. You know, beaches... You know, those places where we fight things?

All I've done with Alan is painted him all over with gouache which is a kind of ready mix water colour-y base paint really. The great thing about it is you can just wash it off even when it's dry. I mean, of all the things I've made on *Art Club*, I have most enjoyed working on Alan.

Protective Spirit Alan
2020

Grayson Perry

Ceramic, metal, stones,
found objects
Courtesy of the artist and
Victoria Miro

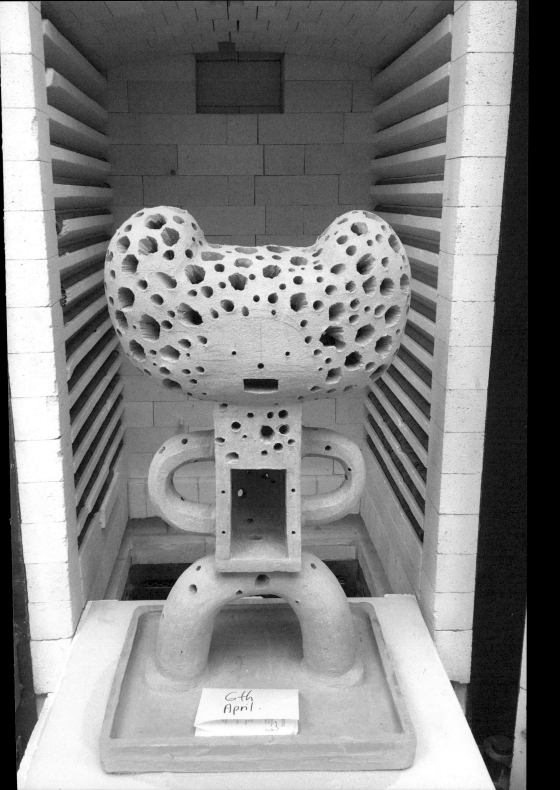

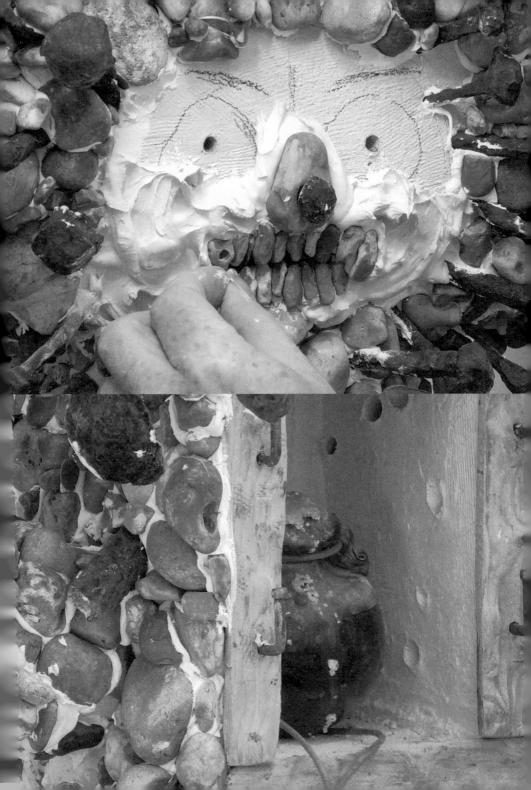

UP THE
KEY
WORKERS!!

Acknowledgements

With thanks to: Channel 4,Swan Films,
Fine Art Transport provided by Jayhawk Ltd.
Shaminder Nahal, Erica Bolton, Manchester
Contemporary Art Fund, Christian Anderton,
Jo & Tom Bloxham, James & Katie Eden,
Mark Garner, Mark & Toni Hawthorn, Thom
Hetherington & Sophie Helm, Alison Loveday,
Sarah Maskell, Lucy Noone Blake & David
Blake, Howard Ratcliffe & Melissa Ratcliffe,
Jeremy & Jane Roberts, Andy Spinoza, Martyn
& Val Torevell

Manchester Art Gallery would also like to
thank: Michael Pollard, Andy Botterill and
Framing Manchester, David Carden, Shamus
Dawes, Kate Day, Martin Grimes, Claire
Grundy, Bev Hogg, Phillippa Milner, Catriona
Morgan, Chris Russell, Catherine Ryan, Sian
Stephenson and all the Gallery team

Air Hugs
Elbow Knocks
Awkward Waving

Manchester Art Gallery